WHO SHE IS

Ruth Yeboah

Flore Publishing

For information contact:
http://www.ruthyeboah.com

ISBN: 978-1-7347726-0-9 (Paperback)
ISBN: 978-1-7347726-1-6 (eBook)
Publisher

Flare Publishing

First Edition: April 2020
Printed in the United States of America.

10 9 8 7 6 5 4 3 2 1

Book Cover design by Kofi Ampong

Dedication

I dedicate this book to my dear husband Foster and my baby girls. Fos, you wrote in your vows that you will support me and make all my dreams come true. It was a promise then, but a reality today. Like a caterpillar, you have watched me morph into a beautiful butterfly. You believed in me enough to challenge me to bring out the best in me. With you, I can try, fail, try again, until I get it right. Baby, I got it right this time. I walked right into my purpose to serve and provide guidance for others. You remain one of a kind, I love you oh so much!

To my daughters Ruth Ethel, and Florence, I thank you for being so unbelievably calm, and sticking to the sleep schedule so I can use my alone time to write this book. I love you both dearly. This is for you!

With Love,
Ruth

CONTENTS

INTRODUCTION

The value of a woman is non-negotiable, yet I meet women daily, who bargain their value. Not knowing your value as a woman can cost you everything, unless you discover your identity.

For over a decade, I have worked with children and women as a child protective specialist and a military domestic violence advocate. Each time I encountered an abused woman, I wondered: "what happened to her?" There was nothing wrong with the women I have met throughout my professional life, but one thing was certain; something happened to these women that caused them to be in this situation right now. I worked diligently to advocate for these women, but I still wanted to figure out what happened. Most times, I couldn't just ask her; "what happened to you" because she had not even connected the dots of her past and her current circumstances.

After years of observation and interaction, one thing became loudly clear: **self-love** was the underlying cure for many of the problems women face today namely domestic violence, low self-esteem, lack of confidence, depression, marital problems, and even financial problems. To truly benefit from this book, I ask that you have an open-mind and willingness to create a paradigm shift as we discuss the most crucial issues women face in life.

This book takes you on a journey of self-discovery, uplifts you to your divine worth, and empowers you to identify or regain your strength as a woman. This is not your typical book; it is a conversation I am having with you from my living room. As you read this, you can see me as your therapist, your coach, your mentor, a friend but most importantly a sister. So, grab your pen or pencil and have a seat with Ruth.

THE SELF CONCEPT THEORY

Who am I?

"Self-concept" is a term coined by social psychologist Baumeister in 1999 to describe a person's belief of who he or she is. The underlying beliefs that a person has of themselves impacts the way he or she views the world. Personal attributes such as self-esteem, self-love or self-worth are all a product of how intact our self-concept is. We develop our self-concept in childhood, based on the way our caregivers or loved ones interacted with us. When a child receives positive responses through positive reinforcement, he or she will develop the tools and coping skills that lead to the confidence necessary to navigate life. However, if a child receives negative feedback or criticism for his or her actions and accomplishments, that child ultimately learns to become critical of themselves and others.

Self-concept is at the root of your self-esteem and confidence building. A damaged self-concept results in long-term effects on your overall mental health and social functioning. Self-concept affects your attachment and trust with others. Most people with low self-esteem have maladaptive coping skills and face issues such as substance abuse, teenage pregnancy, suicide, anxiety, depression, school dropout. Most of our behaviors today can be linked to our self-concept, what we think of ourselves.

The lack of a positive self-concept can be addressed through positive reinforcement or affirmation. The key is to rewrite the narrative you were fed as a child and create a more positive image of yourself.

- What made you who you are today?

_____

_____

- Were you encouraged or put down as a child?

  _____

  _____

  _____

- Were you always punished or disciplined as a child?

  _____

  _____

  _____

FAMILY DYNAMICS

My Narrative

My late grandmother was a huge advocate for family unity. We often hear "blood is thicker than water". I must admit though, as a ninth child of a family of ten, I beg to differ. My grandmother lived for 102 wonderful years on this earth. She was such a loving and happy person. She never once disrespected her siblings, yet they were all so mean to her. She lived free of any major sickness except hypertension. Her life was proof that being good to people has lasting positive results. However, not every family member can be like my grandmother.

There are family members who are jealous, prideful, and hateful. They set out to betray and hurt you out of jealousy; and there are some who wish to always demean you just to appear better than you. They want to control, manipulate, or blame you by playing victim, creating confusion, spiritualizing everything, threatening you, using and abusing you. It is unhealthy to tolerate such family members. There comes a time when you need to separate and keep them at arm's length. The most painful thing I have ever experienced came from my family. You sacrifice so much all in the name of family, meanwhile they are plotting ways to destroy everything you ever worked for. To survive unhealthy family dynamics, you must learn to:

1. Set boundaries

Boundaries are important in any relationship; without boundaries people take you for granted. Period. When people know they can get away with anything, they won't miss a beat, they will do exactly that. Here is a practical example: you lend money to your sister, your brother, or cousin, they don't pay you back. You tell yourself, it's only $50, you brush it off and move on. Months down the line, they "forgot" to pay you back, but they certainly didn't forget that you hold the money bag. So, they present another situation to you, that you can even see how bad they need the money to register their car again or they can't go to work. Again, you oblige, because "family is everything". You thought they learned their lesson to save for a rainy day, but, no they didn't. The third time is a charm, so they come back to you again, for a bigger amount of money. You feel so bad saying no, you offer to give them half. At that, they get really upset with you because "you have the money and don't want to help anybody." At this point you are confused because you are wondering who this "anybody" is, because last time you checked they owed you twice and never paid you back.

When you have a problem with saying no, people will keep taking advantage of you. I bet you this family member dresses better than you when you guys step out because their priorities are all messed up. They spent their money uselessly and use your money to handle what should be their priorities. So, it is now time to set clear boundaries that you would not lend money to family members unless they have shown you that they are trustworthy.

The rule I have adapted for myself is *to only lend money I can afford to lose*. So, if you asked me for money the first time, no repeats with me. I will give you half of anything over $250. So, let's say you need $400, I will only give you $200, knowing that if I don't get it back, I will be fine with it. Once I give you that half, I take it as a seed, I may or may not take it back even if you decide to give it back to me. It is a rule that has worked for both my spouse and I, and that prevents unnecessary arguments with family members. Don't feel pressured to give more than you can afford to lose. Do what you can without twisting your arm, anything beyond that is an obligation.

2. Take a breather

There are times you do all you can to maintain peace and people are not receptive. Conflict arises, you speak with the person and open-up about your feelings; you even forgive them without an apology from them and try to start over with them. They flat out refuse to be mature enough to address the issue with you. They overlook and minimize your feelings. They spend more time going to other family members and friends to talk about you. They want you to feel guilty about something they did to you, instead of apologizing to you. You yearn for them to explain to you why they betrayed you. You fantasize in your mind about how the past could have been different. You want closure of the pain and betrayal, but here is the reality: It may never happen, and you may never know why they hurt you. But you must move on, and not allow things outside of you to impact who you are.

We waste so much energy obsessing about those who have hurt us, but those people don't even care. Why make their feelings your burden? They themselves are wounded and don't understand their pain, so they inflict pain on others. They are the problem not you.

You should cut ties with such people to keep your sanity. It may not be forever, but just until you learn to manage your emotions around those family members. You cannot force a relationship with them just because they are family. You must be OK with their position and not frustrate yourself in the process. Love is a must, but relationship is optional.

Today, in whatever stage you are, on the journey to survive your family, I urge you to take time for yourself, love yourself enough to require a better treatment. Stop believing their negative talks and start walking in what you know to be true. It is possible they have hurt you, betrayed you, spread lies about you, let it go. You have a chance now to be good to yourself so choose you and let go of the past! Forgiveness is imperative when dealing with family. Don't blame yourself for loving or helping them. You did what you thought was right. You did nothing wrong. They wronged you, so you ought to forgive yourself for choosing them over you. Your loyalty was taken for granted so now is time to pull back.

- Does your family put you between a rock and a hard place? Are their demands overbearing?

_____

_____

_____

- Do you deal with your family out of obligation or because you want to?

_____

_____

_____

TRAUMA

What happened to me?

The American Psychological Association (APA) describes trauma as "an emotional response to a terrible event like an accident, rape or natural disaster." Trauma creates lasting effects on individual physical, emotional, and social functioning. There are three types of trauma people face in life, acute, chronic, and complex. Acute trauma results from a single occurrence. Chronic trauma results from prolonged exposure to things like Domestic Violence or child abuse. Complex trauma is being exposed to multiple traumatic events. As a social worker, I have seen the field move into trauma-informed care, where workers are urged to focus on the client's experiences to better assess and serve the needs of the client.

You may ask yourself, "Why am I talking to you about trauma?" That is because we have all been exposed to some form of personal or social trauma. Even if you had a good childhood with no recollection of anything bad happening, you may have witnessed a car accident, or been in an earthquake, or shocked by events like 9/11. Trauma alters your brain as a child and without properly addressing the adverse effects it presents, you may go through life defensive, feeling abandoned, angry, or depressed. Becoming aware of your trauma is the beginning of self-discovery.

When my parents moved to the United States, I was eight years old in the Ivory Coast and was sent to live with my great uncle who was so demeaning and physically abusive to me. One day, he asked me why I was looking at him while he was reprimanding me. Before I could answer, he threw a drinking glass at my forehead. I sustained a huge bump and a small cut on my forehead. This was not your typical glass; it was made from tempered and more durable glass; so heavy the glass did not break when it hit the concrete floor. I spent the next 20 years of my life unable to look directly at people when they spoke with me. Mentally, I registered that looking at adults while they spoke to you was disrespectful. As a student and professional I was unable to look at my professors, bosses, or anyone in authority. Even when I interviewed, I could not make eye contact. I did not acknowledge this trauma until I got exposed to trauma-informed care professionally.

In 1999, at the tender age of 12, I relocated from the Ivory Coast, West Africa to living in the Bronx, NY with my parents. On my way to school one morning, I was robbed at gun point, he snatched my gold chain and threatened me to keep quiet. Even though I was three minutes from my house, I did not even think of returning home. I waited for the bus in panic and anxiously rode the whole hour to my high school. Trauma distorts and alters your thinking. So, even though he did not hurt me physically, I was emotionally traumatized for over a decade, afraid to wear chains or any type of jewelry, and even up to today the mere thought of a gun gives me flashbacks.

Here is the thing, we all have our trauma story if we look deep enough. I know it can be hard letting go of our past trauma, but there must be *a choice to heal.* Trauma impacts who you are. Understand this, you have no control over the past, but you can make different choices today that will change the trajectory of your future. The past should be a place of reference but not where you stay. It is easy to remain a victim to the woes of your past. But I am here to tell you today, that you can improve your life no matter what happened to you. If you have ever been hurt, betrayed, used, or abused, know that it is not your fault. Never think you deserved what happened to you, challenge that crippling thought, it is a lie.

Pain is an inevitable human experience. Pain can cause you to feel worthless, depressed, defensive and just angry. Trauma lies at the core of some of our behaviors, but you must consciously look to connect the dots for healing to begin. We get into unhealthy relationships because of the trauma of our past and don't even know it. So, until you begin to identify who you are and why you do what you do, life will revolve in circles with no clear progress.

We get hurt by people and expect those people to acknowledge the pain they have caused us, we want them to apologize for the pain, so we can have closure. I can't emphasize this enough, hurt people will always hurt others. What if the person who hurt you never says "sorry", would you continue to dwell in the pain and live a life of anxiety, worry and depression? No! You must let go! Forgiveness is freeing, releasing yourself of the baggage is even more exhilarating.

It requires work, and everyone's journey is different. Your memory is your worst enemy in this process, because it will replay vivid memories of the pain, don't give in. Find a positive response to the negative memory you have. You can listen to uplifting music, pray, write in your journal, read, or do anything good that will take your mind off. Some days you will succeed at shaking it off, other days you may not. But don't give up because each day your strength will be renewed. As the saying goes "Never be a prisoner of your past; it was just a lesson not a life sentence."

Remember this: *were you good to yourself when you had the chance to choose you?*

Your parents may have been abusive towards you, neglected you, gave you up for adoption, or used drugs and alcohol around you and missed your childhood. That in turn has caused so much heartache and trauma in your life, impacting your mental health. Your response to the trauma is cutting yourself, or sabotaging your life, ask yourself are you choosing you? Who are you hurting the most?

- Do you have any past unresolved trauma?

_____

_____

_____

- How are you addressing what happened to you?

_____

_____

_____

- Do you believe you can choose to heal?

_____

_____

_____

- Write down what you want to see in your life from today.

_____

_____

BEAUTY AND APPEARANCE

How do I feel about me?

Beauty reflects your inward and outward appearance. They say, "beauty is in the eyes of the beholder." this is very true, but beauty should be how you feel from the inside out. Beauty goes beyond looks. In today's world, the standard of beauty we see in magazines and on TV portrays the stereotypically ideal woman, not your average woman. Yet, many women spend their time, money and energy trying to attain that stereotypically ideal standard. Feeling beautiful in a world that objectifies women is challenging, but every woman should redefine beauty in her own terms and create the appearance that exudes that beauty.

Confidence is beautiful and can be seen in the way you carry yourself. Taking care of your mind, body and soul is essential to your beauty. Before you try to look beautiful for a man or compare yourself to another woman, always ask yourself: do you feel beautiful to yourself? It is not about outsiders, because how you feel about yourself is easily reflected by your choices. Men can spot a woman with a low self-esteem a mile away. You may not even believe it when others tell you, you are beautiful, and so you reject compliments and seek attention in the wrong ways. The wrong man will capitalize on your low self-esteem and hurt you.

Eating disorders, obesity, harsh diets, anxiety and depression are all results of negative body-image. Our childhood experiences, parents and our culture dictate how we view ourselves. The way you feel about yourself affects other areas of your life. So sister, pick yourself up, look in the mirror and smile at the reflection you see. You are beautiful just the way you are, and you are worthy. If you don't believe it, read Maya Angelou's poem "phenomenal woman" until you believe it. You can also practice positive affirmations daily and write them where you can see.

- Do you feel beautiful?

_____

_____

_____

- Do you dress to impress, or do you dress to look good for yourself?

_____

_____

_____

- Are you accepting of your overall appearance (body, mind and soul)?

_____

_____

_____

INSECURITIES

My fears, my worries

Listen, we all have insecurities, or at least had them at one point in our lives. Insecurities transcend class, socio-economic status, marital status, education level, and even beauty. Insecurities impact your confidence level, which ultimately can impact your overall self-esteem. Our feelings of insecurity are masked by and expressed as aggression, defensiveness, hatred, jealousy, over-competitiveness, and shyness. The key is acknowledging that you have insecurities, and then working on turning those insecurities into strengths. When you are insecure about yourself, you settle for less. You allow your job to use you. You may get in the wrong relationship and stay there because you don't think you deserve or can do better.

In relationships, insecurities cause people to work too hard to please others, and still feel inadequate. You may depend on your partner to validate you and become completely dependent on their love and attention. When you begin to feel that your partner completes you, then boundaries have been crossed. What would you do without the relationship or your partner in your life? This can become overbearing for the partner who always must encourage you or seek your approval.

To address your insecurities, you must be honest with yourself and take a step to bring change that will satisfy you. So, if you are insecure about your weight, put things in place to help you lose the weight. If you struggle with bad skin, put in time to research natural remedies that can help sustain healthy skin in the long run not just temporary topical solutions. It is OK to have insecurities, but you must acknowledge them and work on them to develop your self-esteem.

- How confident are you? (List the things that show your own confidence)

_____

_____

_____

- What are you insecure about? Are those things changeable?

_____

_____

_____

LIFE'S PURPOSE

Who am I meant to become?

The Oxford dictionary defines purpose as: "the reason for which something was created or for which something exists." Every person on this earth has a purpose, but one of the greatest tragedies in life is not knowing your assigned purpose. Most people do not accomplish their dreams because of outside influence. Until you begin to walk in your purpose you are like a feather being tossed around by the wind. It goes wherever it is tossed. Purpose creates focus and intentionality. Purpose adds value. In short you cannot live a fulfilled life without walking in your purpose.

Let me explain. Maybe your parents want you to become a nurse, a lawyer, a doctor or an accountant; but you have always wanted to be a teacher or a librarian. Your parents tell you 'teaching doesn't pay', and demand that you do something a bit more prestigious and less bohemian. You are pushed into a field; you care nothing about and struggle unnecessarily.

Your purpose is linked to your assignment. Maybe there are students whose life depend on you becoming a teacher, because that is where they will meet you. My high school teachers played a significant role in both my high school and college education. So, your role would have made a difference in their lives. However, since you chose another field, those students will never get a chance to meet you. If your purpose was to uplift and encourage students you encounter, now you cannot do so. You miss out on your assignment and they miss out on their destiny. It will be difficult for you to live a fulfilled life knowing you are doing something you are not passionate about.

I completed my bachelor's degree from Brigham Young University under three years. I graduated and got a job offer immediately with the New York City Administration for Children's Services formerly known as ACS. Within 6 months of being there, I met an older woman who told me that I was too young and too smart to be in this tough job removing abused children and working late nights. She suggested I attend an accelerated nursing program for a bachelor's in Science in Nursing. Her suggestion appeared harmless and made sense at the time; after all my mother couldn't wait to have one of her kids become a nurse. So, I enrolled in the Nursing program and excelled.

A semester before graduation I realized I was not meant to become a nurse. However, I still owed $40,000 in loans and no degree to show for it. Let me tell you how God works everything out for your good. I got a 76.4 in a very difficult class, and the professor refused to round it up to 77, which was the required grade. This was the lowest grade I had ever received and appealed her decision. I was asked to retake the class. I refused, because it had become so clear to me this was not the path God had for me. Had I been at a 70 or 75 I would have been fine knowing I failed, but I was 0.1 away from making 77. This was a clear sign that could have been easily missed by just retaking the class. I chose to listen to God, and quit Nursing.

Now, most people have no clue what their purpose is. As much as we spend time chasing the wrong thing, we might as well spend time exploring our natural talents and the things that ignite fire in us. Purpose ignites your soul. If you ever had a dream in your heart that never dies and puts a smile on your face every time you think about it, then your purpose is in line with that thirst that cannot be quenched.

You can run away from your purpose if you want, but it will continue to chase you. It is important to do what you are led to do not what others tell you to do. If you are now realizing that you have been doing everything else except what you are supposed to do, then know it is not too late. You can make changes today, if you choose to. The important thing is that you are now aware of it.

Whenever I closed my eyes, I would imagine myself in a suit like my Le Regard suit on the back of this book. I wanted to imagine myself as a nurse, but I could not envision myself in scrubs. It was strange. But over a decade later all the signs were there. I hated the smell of a hospital and got nauseous upon seeing blood. Even though I knew this to be true years ago, I still fell into depression. Through that depression I met my husband. This is a story for another day, but this is how God worked everything out for my good; and every experience thereafter was a building block to this very book, and to who I am.

- Do you know your purpose in life?

_____

_____

_____

- What are you most passionate about?

_____

_____

_____

- What do you imagine yourself doing?

_____

_____

_____

S E L F - C A R E

Time Out!

Caring for others is an instinct for women. As women, we are expected to care for our children, our husbands, our extended families, our friends and take care of the needs of the community (work, church, organizations). Much like other societal expectations of women, it is an unspoken rule for a woman to be of aid to those around her, even at the expense of herself. This brings me to the topic of self-care. Self-care is taking the time you need to attend to you and your needs. A lot of times, we are too exhausted to care about our needs. Can you honestly say you make a conscious effort to take a day to relax, or do something to de-stress or do something you enjoy?

Women tend to sacrifice for others, while neglecting their own needs. Helping others is not a bad thing in and of itself, but when you overlook your own needs and focus on pleasing others; you fall into unnecessary stress. The Merriam-Webster dictionary defines stress as "a physical, chemical, or emotional factor that causes bodily or mental tension and may be a factor in disease causation". This definition makes it clear that stress can make you ill. The normal physiological stress response activates your brain and other bodily functions. However, once the perceived stressor disappears, the body is expected to return to equilibrium. This is not the case for those who are in a constant state of flux: working too much, taking care of family, or having to face other chronic ailments.

Stress also manifests in your behavioral response, your body, your emotions, and your thoughts. Stress can easily trigger heart disease according to the Center for Disease Control & Prevention. Statistics show that most Americans experience chronic stress, hence the increased rate of heart disease. Stress is a public health issue; you must be well before helping others. Take time to fuel yourself.

You cannot fulfill all your expected roles without properly caring for yourself. At some point, you will crash if you do not practice self-care. Self-care is deliberate. Self-care is part of a healthy lifestyle. It means you learn to say no, when you no longer can take on another task. It means you take time out to exercise, meditate, relax, slow down, pray, do nothing, engage in a hobby, intentionally rest, and socialize. Self-care is not taking a day off to catch up on cleaning. Although that is a good thing, self-care means you are doing something for you, to listen to how you feel and to how you are doing emotionally.

- Do you ever take time out for yourself?

_____

_____

_____

- Do you struggle with saying no? If so why?

_____

_____

_____

WHO SHE IS

DATING

Is it meant to be?

The person you choose to date reflects who you are. One way or another, there is a reason why this person appeared on your radar. When you are looking for Wi-Fi, many networks pop up, but knowing that your personal information may be at stake, it is your job to connect to a secure Wi-Fi. In other words, it is your responsibility to ensure that you do not connect yourself to anyone that will demean, disgrace, or disrespect you. But how would I know that? Well, let me help you a bit here but the bulk of the work will need to come from you.

You can date just for fun or you can be deliberate and intentional in your dating. It is important to first ask yourself why you are dating. Is dating the end goal or are you looking to be married to this person? If the answer is marriage, then you need to take a logical approach to this person. Date with your head not your heart. I am not telling you not to fall in love, but I am saying that love alone will not and cannot sustain your marriage. Love requires sacrifice, but most people never get that message because they are rather led by lust. Lust is not love. Feelings are not love. Attraction is not love. Love is independent of external factors, and that is why it is unconditional.

Love requires sacrificial action almost always. You may be the one sacrificing but that is not falling in love, it is a one-way street, you are headed for a ditch. When there is no reciprocity, you are just being desperate. It is important to ask yourself if the person you are dating reflects your values, or do you find yourself changing your values to suit this person in?

There are some non-negotiable values you should consider when dating. In my opinion, the three most important include, your religious beliefs, your attitude to sex and your overall coping skills. Let's consider each in turn.

Religion

You know when you are young, you overlook so many things. You search for love and forget the most important thing in life, your religious beliefs. My faith is the very essence of who I am. I cannot separate my faith in Jesus Christ from who I am. I was not always prayerful or reading my Bible, but I always knew I could not live without it and wanted to raise my children with those teachings. That was a non-negotiable for me. I met people of different faiths who were great men and even knew the Bible and stated that they were willing to convert for me. I was not convinced by their promises and therefore never even ventured to explore that path.

You see, you must know yourself enough to know which risks you can handle. I knew that if they decided later to change their mind, I couldn't do anything about it because I knew their religious beliefs from the beginning. Many told me it doesn't matter, because love will conquer this too, again I never believed it because I knew better. You must be comfortable with the idea that they may never become what you expect. Even as Christians, don't just marry someone because they are in the church. You need to evaluate whether the person lives up to your values. They may not have a personal conviction and might be going to church just because it is what is required from their parents. You need someone who has their own personal testimony. I emphasize faith, because I realize that everything else is built on it. When times get hard, I rely on my faith. But if you are alone in this faith, it will get lonely and frustrating. So, as a single person, you need to determine how important your religion is to you. If you have any inclination that you want a spiritual household, spend time discerning those values and working on your faith prior to jumping in. This is a value system we neglect to pay attention to, but based on my experience has been the key element to holding a marriage together.

- What do you believe in?

_____

_____

_____

- What values can you not live without?

_____

_____

_____

- What are your daily devotional practices?

_____

_____

_____

Sex

I know premarital sex is taboo in some cultures, but a loose topic in many others. I wanted to wait until I was married but fell for the pressures of others demeaning my virginity. Today, sex is expected in dating relationships, both saved and unsaved. I know. I am not telling you that being a virgin will guarantee a good marriage, and neither am I telling you that having premarital sex will secure your marriage. It may or may not have any impact on the security of your marriage but here is what I know. Sex creates intimate bonds that create attachments that are difficult to break if you are with the wrong person.

When you break up with someone you never had sex with, the transition out of the relationship is easier than when you are sexually tied to each other. Sex was meant to seal the deal and consummate a lasting covenant. Unfortunately, not in today's world.

We have taken it for granted today, so we have lost

the value behind sex. Sex is not how you test a relationship. Sex is not how you get a man to stay. Sex is not how you secure a ring. Sex is a sacrificial act between two people in holy matrimony. Anything outside of that can have a negative impact. Why do people date for years, cohabit for years and never marry? Simply because there is a false sense of security and love developed in those relationships. Not many men will date you past a year without sex, even six months if that. Many women in this situation comfort themselves by saying, "marriage is just a piece of paper", "well I know married people who cheat" or better yet "Not everyone wants to be married". It is okay to portray that message, but only you know the truth of what you really want from the relationship. It is easy to date man after man and think sex is normal. But do you take a moment and think about pregnancies, abortions, diseases, etc. Just because you have always had sex while dating, doesn't mean you have to keep having sex.

Do something different and you will see a different result. That man who is not ready for marriage, just tell him you are not ready for sex, and see what happens. It will be painful for him to leave you, but it is better now than wasting years of your life relying on a man who will never marry you. When men see something, they want they go after it, they don't dabble with it.

Believe you are worth more and you will receive more. Once you reach 25 years of age, decide if marriage is something you want. If it is set a hard rule and refuse to date any man pass one year. One year is plenty of time to get to know someone, save enough for a wedding and prepare for life together. This saves you from wasting your youth on a man who clearly had no intention of marrying you from the very beginning. You do not need to be married within a year, but by the 11th month there better be some wedding preparation being made.

Do I want to jump in bed or wait until I am married?

_____

_____

_____

It has been a year of dating, where do you think the relationship is going? If it's been years, then why?

_____

_____

_____

- Do you believe in the reason he has given you for not being ready? If not, why are you still with him?

_____

_____

_____

Coping skills

When we are dating, we are so elated, that we overlook the subtle behaviors that are oh so telling! It is important to know how the other person behaves when they are angry, hungry, sad, stressed, and tired.

- What are the person's coping skills? What happens when they are angry, annoyed, and under pressure?

_____

_____

_____

- Do they rely on smoking, alcohol or drugs to make them feel better?

_____

_____

_____

MARRIAGE

For better or worse?

Marriage is a hot topic for women, whether single, engaged, married, divorced or widowed. Women spend a lot of time talking about their expectations for marriage, yet not many spend time preparing for marriage. The wrong marriage can kill your dreams. What we see today, are elaborate weddings on social media that make it seem as though the most important part of a marriage is the wedding. A survey by Knot.com shows that the cost of an average wedding has increased to approximately $40,000.

We have all been to weddings where we spent more time observing the over-the-top décors, bridal gowns, tuxedos, and venue than paying attention to the vows.

Modern day weddings are so glamourized, you can clearly witness disconnect between the couple's reality of the marriage and the one-day overly expensive event. I cringe at the sight of weddings that leave the couple starting their lives in debt with no savings or property to their name. You may be bombarded by images of wedding after wedding and begin to fantasize about what you see; don't fall for that trap. Make a conscious decision to prepare for the marriage, not just the wedding. The wedding should be a fitting celebration of the start of the rest of your lives together, not a one-off event or "happening."

Society wants to redefine marriage to suit people's lifestyle and choices, but instead of going with the flow, identify for yourselves as a couple the sanctity of marriage and do all you can to protect, preserve and create a marriage that coincides with your purpose. Marriage is a covenant between two people with God at the center. God authored marriage, therefore removing God from marriage is like removing the foundation under a house. The house might stand for some time, but ultimately it will sink.

When a marriage is stable, the children thrive, progress is made by the couple and success is achieved more easily. There are many external factors that contribute to a couple's yearning for marital success, namely modern-day expectations, personal and extended family issues/demands, and finances on top of what matters to God. Marriage is becoming a social contract instead of the covenant relationship God intended. Yours is to ensure you don't succumb to this trend.

Here are some reasons people get married, and how that impacts the overall success of the marriage.

○ *Loneliness*

We all face issues of loneliness, some of those issues stem from the trauma we talked about. Until those issues are resolved or addressed, you will continue to face them. Low self-esteem and abandonment issues cause people to yearn for love and attention. If you find yourself wanting to be with someone just to avoid spending your life alone, you may be battling issues of loneliness. Your spouse is not a therapist, seek help for yourself.

○ *Age*

Women are said to have biological clocks that create

unnecessary pressures to be married. Friends and family are good at also reminding you that the clock is ticking. You dread family reunions because everyone wants an update on how far you are in that process. So, you get pressured to settle for anything. Let me tell you, being married at 40 to the right man is better than settling for just anything at 25 years old.

○ *Love*

There are genuine people who get married because they are in love, however the feeling of love alone will not sustain a marriage. You need friendship, compassion, respect, sacrifice, and loyalty to that individual. You can't tell anyone "in love" about the negative traits of their partner because they are supposedly "blind" and high from that potion, so their logic can even be blurred. Take your time to fall in love, because you will be shocked to see two people who once loved each other try everything in their power to destroy each other during divorce. It is like night and day.

○ *Peer pressure*

There is a tendency for women to get married just

because their friends are all entering the marital nest. It is an unspoken competition that tends to exist with women. Beware because you may be committing yourself to something you don't even want just to feel like you also got a ring. You may have the ring, big, shiny, diamond encrusted, yet cry yourself to sleep every night. Is it worth it?

o *Financial stability*

Some consider marriage a financial plan and do all they can to secure a relationship with a man who can take care of them. Unfortunately, marriage requires more than just money. If you have financial issues work on them now while single, don't wait to burden your spouse.

The decision to marry

I meet women who regret marrying their husbands. They are looking for a way out, because they knew they shouldn't have married him. Pregnancy is not a reason to marry someone. It is a disservice to you when you know not to marry someone yet still force yourself to do so. Ladies, marriage will not and does not complete you if you came into it broken. Your marriage should be unique to you with someone you love, but also share similar values with. When life gets tough the feeling of love seems to vanish, but the values, the friendship, the compassion and care will sustain you. This is how your love grows fonder, through the experiences. Good looks and romance alone will not sustain your marriage. Be conscious of your reasons for getting married, and once married work at it without all the distractions from others.

The architect of your home

Let me tell you, how cunning the enemy is; you yearn for a happy and peaceful marriage. You end up with a good marriage. Yet your unresolved past trauma takes root in that marriage and disrupts the peace by not allowing you to enjoy the marriage. We may not consciously realize this is happening, until it is too late. Fear causes negative reaction in people. So even though you have what you've always wanted, you have insecurities that tell you, the marriage is not what it appears to be. This lie festers and sets up the stage for arguments and chaos in the marriage.

Proverbs 14:1 says "the wise woman builds her house, but with her own hands the foolish one tears hers down". I discussed the issue of trauma because most of us do not recognize how our past dictates our behavior, attitudes, and beliefs. A woman who has trust issues based on her past will enter a relationship and unknowingly smother her husband. She means well, yet still creates situations that only bring chaos to her home.

A woman may also be afraid to be alone, and out of that fear look for reasons that her spouse is cheating on her. I cannot stress this enough; whatever you feed lives, if you feed your imagination with scenarios of your husband cheating, you will start to believe. Listen, if you go looking you will find. Now your suspicions may be confirmed, so you let loose the "crazy" in you and set your own house on fire with arguments and unnecessary fights. OK so maybe you saw a picture, maybe you saw a text or a phone call record, is it possible that you are assuming or judging too quickly? Will that "evidence" provide room for discussion or will that create defensiveness that hinders the ability to "discuss". There is a huge difference between interrogating (accusing) and asking for clarity. Trust is a necessary ingredient.

- What do you do often, ask or accuse? Are you more focused on being right and collecting evidence or are you yearning to create a drama-free home filled with peace and love?

  _____

  _____

  _____

- Why do you want to marry that person? Or why did you marry that person?

  _____

  _____

  _____

- Have you prayed about this man? How do you know he is the one?

  _____

  _____

  _____

- If given a chance to choose again, would you still choose your current spouse? Why or why not?

  _____

  _____

  _____

- Since you are now married to him what are you going to do differently?

_____

_____

_____

- Are up facing a difficult time in your marriage right now? What measures are you taking to address the presenting issues?

_____

_____

_____

MOTHERHOOD

Am I enough?

The role of a mother is so important in the home. Motherhood remains one of the biggest challenges women face. Whether a woman can conceive or struggles with fertility, there are challenges to face. Many cultures expect women to become mothers, in fact women are reared and prepared for motherhood. So, when fertility issues arise, it is debilitating to that woman. People ask you when you will have a child, without knowing the struggles behind closed doors. I want to tell you that you are still a woman and worthy even though you are struggling right now, pray, accept medical interventions, seek help, but most importantly believe that you can have a baby.

For those privileged to be a mother, don't take that role lightly. It comes with a huge responsibility. Don't raise your children out of the pain of your past, allow them to become who God intended them to be. So many mothers try to live vicariously through their children, this is not healthy. It creates unnecessary pressure on you the mom and the child become resentful towards you. Children are individuals who will become adults, raise them with that in mind. Don't project your insecurities on them, and don't associate your values with the behavior of your children.

It is an overwhelming task to become a mother. Parenting should be done by both parents, but unfortunately women do most of the parenting even in two parent families. Today, mothers make up the bulk of the workforce, then return home for the hardest job on the planet. My hats off to you mom.

- Are you instinctively maternal? Are you there for your child or do career demands divide your time?

_____

_____

- Do you discipline or punish your child?

  _____

  _____

  _____

- What legacy am I leaving my children?

  _____

  _____

  _____

INFIDELITY

Traumatized!

Cheating is traumatic, and impacts us emotionally, psychologically and physically. Cheating remains a serious relationship issue in dating and marriage. The cheating partner may or may not realize the level of stress caused to the other partner. However, a single selfish act from one partner can have lasting consequences on the entire family including the innocent children. While cheating is often not discussed outside the marital home or with close friends, it is a concern that plagues many marriages. There is a double standard when it comes to cheating;

it is almost expected and accepted with men, more so than with women. A cheating man is shrugged off as "normalized" behavior, but for a woman it's shameful and stigmatizing.

A partner who has sex with someone other than their spouse damages the foundation of trust that intimate relationships are built on. Surprisingly, it's not often just about sex. Many men and women point to simple lack of affection or an emotional disconnect between them and their partners as the root cause for cheating.

Most often, people look outside for solutions to their marital problems instead of resolving them with their current spouse. Couples fail to communicate their needs, but the reality is some couples don't even know what their needs are. There may be complaints about things on the surface that may not really be the real reason behind the disagreements in the marriage.

Let me explain, the wife asks the husband to take out the trash. The husband is already upset about not having food after returning home from a long day of work. The wife had the kids all day, she is exhausted and although she had intentions to cook a hot meal, she didn't. He is tired and hungry. She is tired and resentful for pausing her life for the kids. Neither of them knows the others pressing needs because they chose to keep it bottled up inside. They both expect the other to know their feelings, and step in to alleviate those feelings, without having to articulate them.

Unfortunately, they are both mentally justified by their feelings, so they choose to be "right" in their mind and do not feel the need to tell the other their feelings. They may reach out to a friend or a family member to complain about their needs. But at no point do they take the initiative to communicate those needs to one another. Here is the danger. Most of the time, men confide in other women (co-workers, old friends, even exes) to make them feel better, whereas women tend to reach out to their girlfriends. Either method is dangerous. Simply because it's a breach of confidentiality and trust and can make things go sour.

The woman listening to the husband may see the wife as lazy and unsupportive to a working husband. She may venture to prove this man that he is a "good man", something he has not heard from his wife. In his mind, she does not appreciate what he is doing for the family by working so hard to provide, because if she did, she would always make sure there is food on the table. I mean this is the least she can do; she is not working. This is a mental conversation the man is having. He may even express that to the other woman "friend". She will agree and the man would begin to see an understanding woman who responds to *his needs*. The man would now rely on the woman for moral support. This can ultimately lead to emotional cheating, at first used for mental escape but can easily result in a romantic and sexual relationship developing as the unintended consequence.

Understand this, a man in this position with no initial intention to cheat on his wife is very vulnerable. The wife in this case also feels justified in dedicating her life to her children by being a stay-at-home mom. She believes when the husband gets home, he should pick up where she left off, and "parent". All she focuses on is her fatigue and the lack of appreciation on his part. She feels instead of him complaining about not having food or having an attitude about doing any chores at home, he needs to "man up". Well, same scenario, different perspectives.

There are reasons that may contribute to infidelity, I say contribute because no one is responsible for your cheating except YOU. There is a tendency to place blame on the other spouse as though they caused the cheating. They may have done things that caused emotional disconnect but, they cannot be blamed for the decision to break your marital vows.

There is intentional cheating, and a woman knows when she has a player on her hands. She knows, but she takes the risk because she thinks she can save the man from himself. Here is the truth. You cannot save a man who has no respect or regard for the sanctity of marriage. So back to our scenario, the man is upset, the woman is exhausted. They are both feeling justified. No one wants to be the bigger person. The emotions keep running wild and their outside emotional support is not challenging those feelings. So, guess what, this fester and becomes cankerous. Both the wife and the husband now seek relief, in the form of addiction, depression, and the most dreaded cheating. The new relationship is exciting and enticing and seems so much more loving than the spouse at home. It is a trap! It is not more fun, or more loving, or better than home. It will give that temporary appearance because your entire focus is on escaping this reality instead of facing your marriage head on.

Most of us have been running our whole life. When we don't like something, we get rid of it. When we meet challenges, we give up on our dreams. When someone tells us the truth, we avoid them like a plague. We just run and quit relationship after relationship. We run in the opposite direction of our destiny, our helpers, and those who love us because they challenge our thought process, and our behaviors. Running delays your destiny. Running procrastinates your need to change.

So, stop running! Face your demons! Deal with the real issues in your marriage and live a liberating life! Relationships are not instant pots. Relationships are slow cookers. They take ample time to warm, simmer, and boil; but the ingredients will mix, tenderize and create succulent juices. Don't underestimate slow cookers, because they take time. Two imperfect people coming together to become equally yoked will require love, mutual respect, and discipline. Those traits are learned not given.

Men cheat because they can, and there are many women who make it easy for them to do so because they are desperate. If a man chose you, he knows why he married you and will stand by it. The reason men cheat is never justified but those reasons matter. Women, we do push men to the edge at times. It is not a pleasant place to be, but it is important to discuss the conditions surrounding the cheating. You do not need to blame yourself, and say you are not good enough as a wife. Never blame yourself. However, a wise woman would inquire about the contributing factors, because they do matter.

Infidelity creates so much discord in marriage but can be overcome together as a couple. You can fall in love all over again, because that negative experience now forces you to rekindle the love you once had in your relationship. That is the bottom line, we stop dating after marriage. We forget and stop doing the little things that cemented the initial bond, the simple affectionate touches, embraces and compliments. The things that made you say "I do" are all forgotten, because we get caught up and stuck in the routines and day to day hustle and bustle of life. You must return to date intentionally again; the pursuit makes life so much more exciting! Whatever the underlying reason for cheating, it is no less devastating to find out that your husband or wife is having an affair.

- No one wants to be cheated on, but if you have experienced infidelity in your marriage, have you recovered and healed from the pain?

  _____

  _____

  _____

- Do you use or threaten infidelity as a bait to get what you want?

  _____

  _____

  _____

- Was your spouse remorseful? Has he shown accountability to rebuild trust?

  _____

  _____

  _____

FRIENDSHIP

Friend or Frenemy

Friendships are created for many reasons. Some become friends with you because of what you do for them, some because you make them feel better about themselves, others because they genuinely care, and some are just lonely. Situations in life will reveal those intentions over time. We spend decades befriending people who may have been dead weight all along, but we were too afraid to get rid of those people because you were too focused on the years spent together. Quantity does not mean quality in any relationship. When you were young, you probably didn't care what your friend had or wore, but as you got older the comparison and competition started with who you dated, married, or even children.

Someone shared with me that when you are going through infertility it is hard to be happy for your friends who are having children. Although I feel for those going through those difficult times, I had a hard time understanding how being jealous or unhappy for the next person would change the situation at hand. Allowing life's challenges to get in the way of your friendship may seem justified to the person suffering, but unfair to the friend who has always been there for you and had nothing to do with your situation. I know this is a sensitive topic but a necessary one because women go through this situation again and again and lose good people who may be in their lives when the time comes for them to celebrate their own children. Just like any challenge in life, becoming bitter isn't the solution.

Women need friends or sisters for talking, sharing life's ups and downs, or simply for venting their frustrations. "Women of Value INC" offers a platform for women to navigate difficult situations like childbirth, parenting, career, and divorce. But also, to celebrate and embrace women's successes.

Maya Angelou once said, "If people show you who they are believe them the first time". There is a tendency to want to mentally rewrite an experience and give the benefit of a doubt to those who blatantly hurt you. It may be because you do not wish to lose them in your life, or you are just comfortable in this relationship and have accepted the mistreatment as normal. Whatever it is, you end up focusing on how long you have been friends with this person and can't seem to accept that they did intentionally hurt you. Jealousy has no place in friendship and should not be tolerated. Jealousy is wanting something that does not belong to you, thinking you deserve it more than they do. You may share a dream with a friend who is so jealous she discourages you. Read between the lines!

There are friends who feel they deserve better than you. No, they won't say it, but they will act like it. So, listen carefully to their response when sharing your personal life! Be wary! Don't become an open book to just any friend! Not every friend is disloyal, resentful or jealous, but when you have a jealous friend that you are loyal to, you need to check yourself and start taking care of you before they lead you to the point of insanity.

- Do you trust your closest friend?

_____

_____

_____

- Are you jealous of your friends, wishing you had something your friend has?

_____

_____

_____

- Are you a loyal friend?

_____

_____

_____

DOMESTIC VIOLENCE

I deserve better!

Domestic violence is like the pink elephant in the room. It is so rampant, yet there is little or no conversation about it. It is a public health concern, and impacts children in negative ways. It is a vicious cycle, and most children who experience violence in the home become victims, not only scarred by the experience, but also becoming abusers themselves. One of the questions outsiders ask victims pertains to why they stay in such relationships. Fear, shame, lack of financial stability and custody tend to be the leading reasons people remain in abusive relationships.

I spent six years working as a domestic abuse advocate for the Air Force. Both men and women are abused, but over 90% of my clients were women. First, if you or anyone you know is being abused, you can't blame them because the perpetrator chose her, not the other way around. Abusers prey on people's weaknesses, and when you are "in love" you overlook so many things. One out of every three women will be a victim of domestic violence in her lifetime. Domestic violence can be physical, verbal, financial or sexual. Perpetrators of violence thrive on isolation. They manage to remove your support system from you, it is a subtle process. You must beware and remain alert when you meet someone who intentionally causes a rift between you and your family or friends. It is an attempt to isolate you. Without support, you lose yourself much faster and make them the center of your world. Domestic violence doesn't discriminate, it can happen to anyone regardless of economic status, educational background, age or race. Strangulation is a deadly force often applied by the abuser in such violent situations, it can silently kill and maim. If you are ever strangled seek medical attention immediately, because it can have a long-term impact on your body.

Abuse thrives on silence; so, speak out, get help before it is too late. Do not make excuses, violence in the home is not an anger management issue, it is a control issue. People do not just stop abuse; they need and must get outside professional help and counseling.

Abusers are so busy blaming you for their behavior, they do not stop and acknowledge their problem, which means they won't seek help. Your job is not to "fix" them. Women love to be saviors to men. It is not your job! I can't emphasize that enough. Yes, they went through a horrible childhood, but you cannot heal their past.

Here are some red flags to look out for. Abusers rush you into love. Maybe you just met a guy, after a couple of dinners they want to get serious. They make you believe you are the best thing that has ever happened to them, and don't want to lose you. They may ask for sex early, jump into a serious dating relationship or marriage quickly. They talk about moving in with you after a few encounters. Before you have a chance to think and process your emotions, they bombard you with more serious requests. That is a red flag, run! They may in a subtle way text and call you every time you are away from them. Now if you are someone who has abandonment and attachment issues, it may seem super cute at first, before you realize you are reporting your daily itinerary to them. They may even surprise you at work, it is cute until you realize they are just there to check up on you. Abusers are extremely jealous and accuse you of cheating constantly. Remember if they can't have you no one else can, so they make you believe no one else will want you; so that is why they must demean and degrade you. You are an adult, no one should tell you how to dress, where to go, where to work, and who to be around. If it doesn't feel good or it makes you uncomfortable, then know it is not right. Slow things way down and see their reaction that will be telling.

- Are you experiencing domestic violence in your current relationship?

_____

_____

_____

- What factors impact your decision to stay?

_____

_____

_____

- What resources do you need to safely leave the abusive relationship?

_____

_____

_____

- Have you told family and close friends? (It is for accountability).

_____

_____

_____

PERSONAL SAFETY

Protecting myself

Let's be honest there are so many things women worry about that men never lose sleep over. Personal safety is one of those things. Date rape is real and happens in high school and college settings more often than we care to admit. It is true that what you wear is not a reason to be violated, but the reality is that you cannot control what others do. So, it is your prerogative to protect yourself. As a college student, I watched other young ladies run to and from campus in the wee hours of the night. I always used to cringe because there is a false sense of safety on college campuses where students think that everybody on campus is there to learn. Campuses are so big and accessible that you truly never know who is, who. You go out partying and trust your friends to look after you and they don't. You decide to go off with a guy and the unthinkable happens. Sister you must protect yourself. Don't easily trust a stranger.

Years ago, I met a guy through job training. We started to get to know each other. Then one day he invited me over to his house, he said he was going to order in food. After we ate, he asked to massage me. I don't know if I succumbed to the massage, because I was afraid, he might ask for more or whether I left my brain at home. Whatever it was I laid down and he proceeded to massage me. A few minutes in, I noticed he was getting super comfortable while I was super uncomfortable. I softly told him, this is so good, and I am so impressed, but can we do this another night because I am not feeling well. I immediately put on my shirt and left. On the way home, I realized how vulnerable I had made myself.

We live in a social media age where technology rules every area of our lives. We meet people online every single day, and some of us take the initiative to meet those people face to face without any precautions. It is great to meet new people, but you always must think safety first.

Growing up my worst fear was being raped. At the tender age of eight, in my grandmother's yard in the Ivory Coast, my cousin ran to me crying and bleeding everywhere. I asked her what happened to her, she told me that she was going to the night market and a man pulled her to a dark alley and raped her. I told some adults and we ran back to the market and found this man. He was caught and let go within minutes, because someone came and said this is no big deal. My cousin was taken to the hospital and was told she won't be able to have children. He left her tremendously scarred that will stay with her forever due to the physical, psychological, and emotional damage he caused her. She was also eight years old.

While in college I met a guy online. Eventually we became friends and years down the line we went out to eat a couple of times. One day he asked me for a ride, once I got to his house, he asked me to come in so he can grab something quick. I told him if he is only grabbing something quick, there is no need for me to go inside. He convinced me. I thought his mom was home as usual, so I went in with him. As soon as the door shut behind me, he came for me. I asked him what he was doing, and he said you already know. You have heard of flight or fight, or freeze. I had to decide in a split second, but I was not going to let him have his way. I fought him, physically, and pushed him to the hall and quickly opened the door and ran for my life. After that it was awkward for a long while, we are no longer friends. But I was one of the lucky ones. Everyone reacts to shock differently.

A strictly platonic friendship is hard to have between men and women. How many of you had a guy friend who liked you, who was a friend with benefits or who just won't give up chasing after you. It seems flattering but super annoying at the same time. So, ladies, be safe and don't expect others to prioritize your safety.

- How do you maintain your safety?

_____

_____

_____

PERSONAL FINANCES

Am I ready for a rainy day?

In school we are taught how to count money, but not how to handle money. At 18 years old, credit card companies used to come looking for you to give you credit. As a college student if your parents did not teach you how to use money, you get trapped into absurd credit card usage for eating, dressing, and chilling. Only to later discover you must pay it all back. Financial ignorance can be so costly and can take decades to resolve. Your parents didn't know about money, so they didn't teach you. You fall into the vicious cycle and now you become a slave to the dollar because you must now spend the next 20-30 years paying back for the lack of knowledge.

Managing your money has little to do with how much you make, and everything to do with discipline. It is imperative that you arm yourself financially for a rainy day. Since school did not teach us financial education, they would not teach our kids. It is our job to show them how to work, save, budget, invest, and secure their future through life insurance and other investments. College students leave college with insurmountable student loans and spend the next 20-25 years of their lives trying to stay afloat. Is that prestigious college degree worth it if there are no scholarships involved? You must look at the whole picture, with financial freedom in mind.

The goal as a single person, should be to live within your means, spend less, and save as much as you can. They tell you credit cards are good for emergencies, ask yourself how many of the expenses on your credit cards are for emergencies? Think about it, if you spent only on the necessities of life you could have enough money to cover the things you did not expect. Unfortunately, most people get caught up living beyond their means, by trying to impress people who do not even matter.

Your money habits as a single person transfer into your marital home. Money is the leading cause of problems in marriages, yet most couples never even discuss finances prior to marriage. It is often overlooked because people are often delusional in the dating stage. Here are some significant questions to ask your spouse to be.

- Do you save? If so, how much income should be set aside for a rainy day?

_____

_____

_____

- Do you pay your bills on time?

_____

_____

_____

- Do you wish to rent or buy? If so, how much should your mortgage be?

_____

_____

_____

- Should we pull our credit together?

_____

_____

_____

- Do you need that brand-new car at this stage of your life? Can you afford it?

_____

_____

_____

- What are your needs vs. your wants?

_____

_____

_____

- What are your financial goals? What income level do you need to fulfill career and life ambitions?

_____

_____

_____

- When do you wish to retire?

_____

_____

- How do you envision your life financially?

_____

_____

_____

- Do you invest in yourself, to buy books, attend seminars, or get a coach?

_____

_____

_____

I hope that these questions will begin the much-needed conversations couples miss during dating and prevent money becoming an impediment in your future life together.

OVERCOMING LIFE'S CHALLENGES

Resilient as a fortress

Life is so full of challenges, but we cannot dwell in those dark moments of our lives. We must overcome to live a more fulfilling life. Change is an inevitable part of life and is to be expected and embraced rather than dreaded. Change can be challenging, but that is where growth lies. We all want to be happy, and thus associate our happiness to things around us. The true essence of happiness is to have inner joy independent of external factors. It is to have peace despite the storm around you. We experience pain and betrayal, as uncomfortable as that may be, they are necessary. Most of the greatest achievements in life originate in adversity or from a place of pain. Trying to avoid pain is like trying to prevent a child from growing. They may not mature but they must grow. There are things in life better learned the hard way through experience. We try to skip over these experiences, until you learn the lessons that are meant for you, some things will keep recurring to you. No one is exempt, you must go through the process life tailors for you. Everyone's path is different, but the message remains the same. You must overcome barriers to get your breakthrough. Your job is to discover ways that can ease your process of becoming. Your experience will shape the ideal you. So instead of "why me?" you should be asking, "What lessons do I need to learn from this?" As unpleasant as it may be, you must look beyond the ongoing crisis or circumstance and figure out the lesson. Some people remain in crisis mode because they miss the lessons and focus on the hardships much longer than expected. Some people never even get out of the hardship. Remember, everything in life is a choice. You cannot control others' behavior, but you own your response to everything.

For me prayer and reading my Bible have been my anchor in every challenge I have faced. I do not always feel like praying when I should, but I will recite the word or sing a worship song. There have been times, I was numb to pain and betrayal, so I played music and listened to sermons. I couldn't get myself to do anything. But those small actions revived my spirit. Something as insignificant as watching funny videos can break a smile and improve your mood. Your job is to find out healthy ways to cope with challenging times, so you finally see the light at the end of that dark tunnel. Resilience awaits after emerging from the tunnel.

These questions will help you develop healthy coping skills.

- Do you have hope that things can improve?

_____

_____

_____

- Do you feel that life is about luck or what you make of it?

_____

_____

_____

- What do you do under extreme stress?

_____

_____

_____

- Have you given up on life right now?

_____

_____

_____

- Write down what you would like to see differently in your life right now.

_____

_____

_____

_____

About the Author

Ruth Yeboah received her bachelor's degree in Psychology from Brigham Young University in Utah in 2007. She graduates from Widener University's Master of Social Work program in May 2020. She started her career with the New York City Administration for Children's Services (ACS) as a Child Protective Specialist (CPS) and continued within the foster care system as a Case Manager, working with young children and teen moms. Ruth has over 13 years of experience in trauma and child abuse/neglect. She is a nationally certified Victim Advocate and worked for the United States Air Force in that capacity.

Her experiences denote the core of her philanthropic heart, serving women in need in the United States and West Africa.

In 2017, she founded Women of Value INC, a non-profit organization focused on enriching the lives of women. Ruth is dedicating her many talents to ensure women can identify and fulfill their divine purpose. She is also the designer and owner of Le Regard Apparel, a revolutionary nursing line that can be worn for breastfeeding and post-partum.

Acknowledgments

I thank God for being my shield and my strength every single day of my life. His favour kept me. I thank my dear husband Foster Yeboah, for believing in me enough to challenge me to live out my dreams daily. To my spiritual father, Prophet Atsu Manasseh, I thank you for the practical lessons you taught me over the past decade. You taught me that every challenge provides a reason to worship God the more, and that's where victory lies.

I remain grateful for my sisters Marie Quansah, Dorcas Larbi, and Jeanne Atanga and their supportive husbands for being part of this incredible journey.

To my Brother Tatchie, and other siblings, I thank you for shaping my life.

I remain grateful to my wonderful parents Bishop and Mrs. Frimpong Manso for always praying for me and covering me spiritually.

To my prayer warriors, Pastor Doris Asante, Minister Rose, and sister Priscille, I thank you.

I thank my editor in chief Mr. Alastair Tucker for succinctly capturing the essence of this book.

To Kofi Ampong, I thank you for designing such a phenomenal book cover.

To all my phenomenal Women of Value who believed in me and allowed me to share my gift and knowledge with them in workshops, retreats, and conferences, thank you.

I am grateful for you my readers, for embarking on this self-discovery journey with me. I hope this book provided the platform to reflect, reassess, forgive, and take action to change your narrative.

Please write and share your review on Amazon and tag me on social media.

Follow me on:
Instagram: **@theruthyeboah**
Facebook: **Ruth Yeboah**

Contact Me:
Email: **theruthyeboah@gmail.com**
Phone: 914-265-4050
www.ruthyeboah.com

www.ingramcontent.com/pod-product-compliance
Lightning Source LLC
Chambersburg PA
CBHW021421090426
42742CB00009B/1207